A Big Mess

by Holly Harper

illustrated by Lucy Neale

OXFORD
UNIVERSITY PRESS
AUSTRALIA & NEW ZEALAND

Kevin is up.

3

Kevin will fix it.

The duck is in the jacket.

The cat is on the bin.

Mud is on the rug.

Jen is up.

Jen will fix it.

Jen has the mop and
the bucket.

Mum is up.